JUST DANCE

Spotlight on Ballet

Mel Hammond

Lerner Publications ◆ Minneapolis

Lerner Publications Company
An imprint of Lerner Publishing Group, Inc.
241 First Avenue North
Minneapolis, MN 55401 USA

For reading levels and more information, look up this title at www.lernerbooks.com.

Main body text set in Mikado.
Typeface provided by HVD.

Designer: Mary Ross

Library of Congress Cataloging-in-Publication Data

Names: Hammond, Mel, author.
Title: Spotlight on ballet / Mel Hammond.
Description: Minneapolis, MN : Lerner Publications, [2025] | Series: Just dance (Lerner sports rookie) | Includes bibliographical references and index. | Audience: Ages 5–8 | Audience: Grades K–1 | Summary: "Readers put on their ballet slippers and discover the exciting world of ballet dancing. They will discover what dancers wear and get ballet tips and fun facts. Then readers learn how to plié"— Provided by publisher.
Identifiers: LCCN 2023034481 (print) | LCCN 2023034482 (ebook) | ISBN 9798765625644 (library binding) | ISBN 9798765628829 (paperback) | ISBN 9798765633960 (epub)
Subjects: LCSH: Ballet dancing—Juvenile literature. | Ballet—Juvenile literature.
Classification: LCC GV1787.5 .H35 2025 (print) | LCC GV1787.5 (ebook) | DDC 792.8—dc23/eng/20230722

LC record available at https://lccn.loc.gov/2023034481
LC ebook record available at https://lccn.loc.gov/2023034482

Manufactured in the United States of America
1-1009973-51898-11/1/2023

Table of Contents

Chapter 1

Welcome to Ballet

Get ready to bend, twirl, and leap! Ballet is a type of dance. Ballet dancers flow from one pose to another.

**Some ballets tell a story.
Dancers play characters.**

★ Fun Fact ★

The Nutcracker **is a famous ballet.**

Ballets are often performed on stages. You can also see ballet in online videos.

Chapter 2

Getting Ready

Ballet dancers practice in tight clothes that can stretch. They wear leotards or shirts with tights.

Dancers wear ballet slippers or pointe shoes. They should fit snugly.

Most ballet words are in French!

A ballet studio has wooden floors, mirrors, and a barre. Students dance to classical music. But other kinds of music may be used too.

Chapter 3
What to Expect

At ballet lessons, dancers stretch and warm up. They practice ballet positions at the barre. They practice steps, turns, and jumps.

Teachers help dancers improve.

At the end of class, students curtsy or bow to thank their teacher.

★ **Tip** ★

Drink water! Ballet is hard work.

★ Up Close! ★

How to Plié

- Touch your heels together. Point your toes out.
- Bend your knees. Keep your upper body straight.
- Stand up tall. You've done a plié!

Chapter 4

Putting on a Show

Ballet dancers practice so they can perform. They dance for an audience on stages. When a show is over, the audience claps.

Shows are hard work but a lot of fun! Would you like to try ballet?

★ Fun Fact ★

Many dancers wear a tutu in shows. A tutu is a skirt made with layers of fabric.

Glossary

barre: a bar that ballet dancers hold onto while warming up

classical music: music played with wind and string instruments, usually without words

leotard: a piece of clothing that fits tightly and covers the body

pose: the position that someone stands in

Learn More

Lanier, Wendy Hinote. *Ballet*. New York: AV2, 2021.
Peters, Katie. *Dance: A First Look*. Minneapolis: Lerner Publications, 2023.
Sterling, Holly. *Ballet Kids*. Somerville, MA: Candlewick, 2022.

Index

Photo Acknowledgments

Image credits: Masafumi Nakanishi/Getty Images, p. 5; Aaron Chown/Alamy, p. 7; Julie Lemberger/Getty Images, p. 9; Catherine Ledner/Getty Images, p. 11; Klaus Vedfelt/Getty Images, p. 13; photobac/Getty Images, p. 15; kali9/Getty Images, p. 17; JackF/Getty Images, p. 19; Kseniya Starkova/Getty Images, p. 21; Arctic-Images/Getty Images, p. 23. Design elements: Kilroy79/Getty Images; Iuliia Mashinets/Getty Images.
Cover: Eternity in an Instant/Getty Images.